A Walk Through Time

A Photographic History

of

Market Bosworth

COMPILED BY GLYNIS OAKLEY AND JOAN TOMLINSON

ACKNOWLEDGEMENTS

Thanks to the generosity of local people who have loaned postcards and photographs to add to the already extensive personal collection, it has been possible to produce this book. Not only have the images been forthcoming but the related information has also enhanced the text. The use of the scanner and printer to produce the book has been invaluable and thanks must go to the Market Bosworth Society and the Heritage Lottery Fund for the use of this equipment.

Thanks also go to the Bosworth 2001 group who published "From an Open Wooded Hilltop" and who forwarded a loan to enable this book to be published. "A History of Market Bosworth" by Peter Foss has also been a valuable historical resource.

Glynis Oakley and Joan Tomlinson
2008

ISBN 978 0 9529639 3 0
Printed in Great Britain by Reprico Ltd
2008
Copyright Glynis Oakley 2008

Front cover photograph
The cottages that once stood on Barton Road opposite the Free Church.

Back cover photograph
Wheatsheaf Courtyard 2008

Frontispiece
Park Street 1923

CONTENTS

The Coat of Arms of Market Bosworth Rural District Council reflects the history of the town by incorporating details of the emblems from the arms of families associated with the district. The White Boar symbolises Richard III and refers to the Battle of Bosworth 1485.

"The whole life of man is but a point in time - let us enjoy it."

Plutarch 46AD - 120AD

A WALK THROUGH TIME

A PHOTOGRAPHIC HISTORY OF MARKET BOSWORTH

"A collection of photographs, spanning more than a century, of life in a small town in the centre of England should be shared". This was the comment made when the wealth of photographic history of the buildings and people of Market Bosworth was revealed.

The main purpose of this book is, therefore, to share some of the photographs that are hidden in collections in the homes of local families and in the wider community. The main focus of the architectural pictures is to illustrate some of the changes that have taken place and some of the buildings that have remained unchanged. Making the centre of the town a Conservation Area in 1974 has ensured that the wealth of its architectural history will be secured for future generations. In addition to its historic buildings, there have been people who have influenced the development and character of Market Bosworth, thus the last section, "The Essence of Market Bosworth".

The photographs take you on a journey from the Market Place and down each street, like spokes from a wheel radiating from its hub, and move in a clockwise direction beginning with Main Street.

The most impressive, and perhaps most important buildings, Bosworth Hall, Dixie Grammar School and St Peter's Church, have been given their own sections in the book as thay have had the longest and most colourful history and each in their own way dominate the first impressions of the town.

This book is a photographic history with short pieces of text giving some details about the pictures. It is intended mainly as "A Walk Through Time" giving a glimpse into life of the small market town through the camera lens.

Illustrated here are the houses on the corner of Main Street and the Market Place as they were in the early 20th century. Note the bricked-up windows dating from the days when a window tax was imposed. The window style has been changed over the years with two windows above 3 Market Place having been reinstated and a shop front installed.

In the above photograph, dated 1928, the butcher's shop had an open front which was adjacent to the slaughter house access to the rear of the property. Bill Lampard was the proprietor at this time. Further alterations were subsequently made to the shop, as the top photograph on the opposite page illustrates. Ownership of the shop passed to Bill's son, Jim, in 1967 when the present shop layout was created.

Jim Lampard outside the shop with a Christmas window display in 1954.

One of six inns that existed in Market Bosworth was The Wheatsheaf Inn, which in the survey of 1588 was referred to as The Inn with the Sign of the Unicorne. The oldest parts of the building date back to the 16th century.

THE WHEATSHEAF INN

The courtyard, accessed through the central carriage entrance, provided stabling at one time. There was a saddlers here as recently as 1983. The courtyard has housed many small businesses - including a bookshop, wool shop, travel agents, children's clothes, hairdresser, cafe, accessories shop and a printers.

CENTRAL CAFE

CENTRAL CAFE

In 1926 Mr and Mrs W J Hatton purchased The Wheatsheaf Inn and converted it to the Central Cafe. The ground floor accommodated a high class confectioner's, a gentlemen's hairdresser's and a cafe. The Function Room on the first floor seated up to 200 customers, some of whom are pictured above. It also provided the venue for several organisations - the Women's Institute, the Free Church and Toc H. Many cycle clubs used the Cafe and it was also one of the first in the area to sell ice cream which was made from powder imported from America. Mr Bill Hatton, on becoming Lord of the Manor, collected a 6d fee for parking in the Market Place.

POST OFFICE

The bow fronted property, 9 Market Place, was once the Post Office and the Postmaster, Mr Wright, sold sets of Tuck's postcard views of Market Bosworth as illustrated.

THE OLD BLACK HORSE INN

The photograph above shows The Old Black Horse Inn and adjacent cottages in the 1920s. An elm tree was located here, as were the village stocks. The original building was designed with two gables, then a third was added to create a more impressive facade. The adjacent cottages date back to the early 18th century and were incorporated into the public house in the 1960s. Until recently it was one of the most popular hostelries for local residents but is now a thriving restaurant.

17TH CENTURY THATCHED COTTAGES

These 17th century Grade II listed cottages are now owned by the Borough Council and were "... donated in 1966 to the Rotary Club ... by Arthur James Pickering ... to provide residence for the elderly ... the property was transferred to the local authority in 1975". The cottages are timber-framed with brick infill on a Carlton stone plinth.

This late 18th century corner cottage has changed little other than the re-siting of the doorway and style of the windows.

This is a photograph of the Market Place from Sutton Lane showing, on the left, the bay windows of the Police House built in 1848. The local police officer and his family would have occupied the property, but it is now privately owned. Note the Co-op building in the background with its complete set of chimneys, (a pair of chimneys have since been removed), and the steps on the corner cottage in their original position.

To the left, adjacent to the Police House, was the property which later became Insley & Long butchers. This building was demolished when the new Midland Bank (now HSBC) was built in 1974. An elm tree adorned the Market Place and can be remembered up until the 1930s.

This postcard, dated 1919, shows the building, now owned by the Hinckley & Rugby Building Society, when it was a private dwelling. T Flavell & Sons, solicitors, and the Parish Council now occupy offices in this building. Surveying all is Fred Proudman, gravedigger, bellringer and employee of H Beck & Son.

This view of the Market Place was taken in 1964 from the Dixie Grammar School. The pot holes and the poor state of the cobbles show the condition of the square prior to restoration by the Parish Council in 1991. Ownership of the Market Place has never been established. A Market Charter was granted in 1285 by Edward l and in 1665 passed to Sir Wolstan Dixie.

The Atherstone Hunt meets regularly in the Market Place and is seen here in front of Chapman's Saddlery and the gabled cottages, which were once part of the Bosworth Estate. The facade of these cottages dates from the late 19th century and the ornate barge boards of 8 Market Place were decorated at the time of Charles Tollemache Scott.

This event was possibly a church procession walking in front of what was then H Beck & Son builder's yard. This corner is now occupied by the Clock Shop and Peppercorn Cottage Delicatessen.

Possibly the first Armistice Day Remembrance Service after the erection of the War Memorial in 1920.

These three properties fronting on to the Market Place still stand. The property to the left of the photograph is now The Clock Shop. In the centre is Richmond House with shutters and the delightful addition of the family in the doorway. The property on the right, now Softley's Restaurant, at one time fronted on to Litchfield Street, now Station Road. The houses were built in the early 19th century.

A May Fair was held annually in the Market Place for three days from the first Thursday in May. The celebrations were enjoyed here until the late 1950s.

Records of a school in Market Bosworth go back to the early 14th century. Details of the existence of a Grammar School during Elizabethan times have been recorded. A new Grammar School opened on 27th April 1829 under the headship of Dr Benoni Evans. The lithograph above of the school was drawn by a former pupil, S S Baxter, in 1840.

Dr Evans' main aim for the school was to educate boys, mainly boarders, for university entrance at an anuual fee of thirty guineas. However, Governors were encouraging the education of local boys and John Edwards, a long serving teacher, taught some ninety local boys until his retirement in 1855. The plaque above the mock Tudor entrance door states in Greek, "....Education is a possession of which mortal man (once he has got it) cannot be deprived". The photograph is dated 1906.

THE LONDON CITY AND MIDLAND BANK

THE LONDON CITY AND MIDLAND BANK

The Bank was built in 1904 by H W Beck and Son of Market Bosworth. The photograph shows the building nearing completion with employees and residents in the foreground.

Seen here is a meeting of the Atherstone Hunt in the Market Place before the construction of the Bank. To the rear of the Co-operative store can be seen the house which, at one time, was the home of the store manager.

To the left of the photograph is a row of Grade II Listed Buildings. In the foreground, with the awning, is the shop that is now the Co-op Lateshop.

This photograph taken in 1908 shows 3 Main Street, which is a private residence and a Grade II listed building. The 18th century Georgian facade hides a much older building thought to be 16th century and timber-framed. The remaining buildings have historically been retail outlets. The shop with the awning was Fletcher's Bakery. The bakehouse was located in the adjacent jitty. Quincey's General Store, then Tebutt's Delicatessen and Bamford's Store and Coffee Shop were located at 9-11 Main Street. The property to the right, that is now Michaelmas House, was once the local chemist.

The building on the corner of Park Street and Main Street once housed the Council Offices and the Magistrates' Court. The newsagent now occupies part of the building. On the right, the site of the present post office, Perry's Cycle shop can be seen and in the right foreground was where the Trivetts had a butcher's business. The slaughter house was sited to the rear of Ye Olde Red Lion Hotel. The photograph is dated 1915.

The Regency facade of The Dixie Arms Hotel was constructed in front of the 16th century Bull's Head Inn and it was renamed The Dixie Arms Hotel in 1824. The above photograph, taken in 1904, illustrates the firm's outing arranged by the George Oliver Boot & Shoe Company, based in Leicester.

16

This 1906 photograph shows the Willshee late Drackley grocery store window prepared for Christmas. The Drackleys were a prominant local family during the 19th and 20th centuries. The site is now occupied by Elizabeth Ann Hairdresser's and Lloyd's Chemist. The photograph, top right, shows Quincey's store window decorated for the Coronation of George VI and Queen Elizabeth.

This early 20th century photograph shows a group of ladies outside the row of Victorian terraced houses. On the left is a row of frameworkers' cottages which have now been demolished and replaced by the late 20th century town houses, except for the one cottage incorporated into Ye Olde Red Lion Hotel.

Long's, the butchers, delivery cart is outside the shop that was adjacent to the Dower House. Sausages, a weighing machine, a leg of lamb and a pig's head can be identified on this photograph dated 1906. Their slaughter house was located at the end of the row of cottages in Barton Road.

The Dower House, viewed from Church Street, was built during the period 1760 to 1780 but re-modelled in the 19th century. It stands on the site of The George Inn, the cellars of which still exist below the Dower House. The house also accommodated night staff from the Infirmary. To the right is the Malt House demolished in 1965 to allow widening of the road.

Ye Olde Red Lion Hotel is the oldest pub in Market Bosworth, being built around 1650. It was given a new facade at the end of the 19th century. The Trivett family were publicans for over a hundred years, brewing their own beer, which was distributed to other publicans and also in barrels to local farms. Leicester based Hoskin's Brewery later took over the pub, serving their highly acclaimed real ale.

Above left is a copy of a very early advertisement, prior to the late 19th century alterations. Above right is a Trivett's beer mat from their Osbaston hostlery which they bought in 1899.

Illustrated here is the Malt House, built of Carlton stone around 1690, during the disconnection of electricity prior to demolition in the spring of 1965.

This row of fourteen three-storey terraced houses was demolished in the mid 1930s. They were sited below the Malt House and opposite the Free Church and Mooreland House. Life was difficult in these houses, heated by coal fires and lit by paraffin lamps. The communal pump was situated at the bottom of the road near Long's slaughter house.

The Grey House is a Grade II Listed Building. Behind the 19th century facade built in 1830 stands a timber-framed farmhouse, dating back to the mid 16th century. This property was once part of Home Farm which is sited on Barton Road. Adjoining this is the Red House, also Grade II listed, which was built in 1812 and during the 1820s was an independent school.

On the right is Beech House, built in 1818 with parts dating back to the 18th century. The house was further extended in the late 19th century. It was home to the local doctor during the 20th century and is now Schwiening's Language School.

These are recent photographs of Bosworth Hall gates and St Peter's Church gates. The gates, shown above, form the access to St Peter's Court, now residential apartments, but when built in the 1930s accommodated the nurses who worked at the Bosworth Park Infirmary. St Peter's Church gates, commissioned by Mr W Beck, are illustrated below and were made by Clem Phillips at The Forge, Park Street in 1969. Incorporated into the design are the keys, held symbolically by St Peter, as the founder of the church.

The above stones marked the boundary of Church Cottage (now Holy Bones) and Bosworth Estate and are sited just inside the church gates. Samuel Hunt Perry purchased Church Cottage around 1903 and marked the boundary of his land, charging a toll for passage to the Church. Charles Tollemache Scott followed suit by placing a stone on the Estate side.

Above is Holy Bones cottage. A plaque dated 1861 bearing the Dixie snow leopard has been installed over the doorway though whether this is the date of the building is not known. Samuel Hunt Perry bought the house in the early 20th century, it having been an Estate house prior to that date.

This view of Park Street dates from the late 1940s. On the left is Ye Olde Red Lion Hotel where, not only was beer brewed, but also in 1919, petrol was sold from the handpumps on either side of the entrance to the yard. In the photograph, bottom left, a 1930 Ford Model A is towing a Model T Ford car, minus tyres, away from the Hotel's garage forecourt.The cottages on the right of the above photograph still remain. The premises nearest the junction with Main Street were occupied by W Shepherd & Company, a cycle shop. Seen below right are the cycles displayed for an exhibition in the Club Room at The Dixie Arms Hotel. Unfortunately, in 1907 a fire damaged the shop premises.

W. Shepherd & Co's, Cycle Exhibition, Market Bosworth.

These cottages still remain except for the one on the far left which was a carpenter's shop owned by Mr Armson, who also made coffins as and when required. The shop opposite the end of Park Street is now the Post Office.

This interesting photograph was taken in the yard of The Dixie Arms Hotel. Some of the characters could be carpenters and possibly the dreymen taking a well deserved break as well as the blacksmith, Jack Skelton.

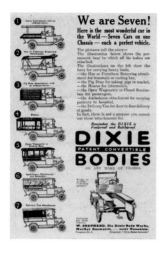

The poster and photograph above advertised Mr W Shepherd's garage at the rear of The Dixie Arms Hotel. He imported Ford chassis onto which a wooden Dixie Body could be fitted. The car was a four seater saloon and could be converted into a van or open truck. The garage closed during the 1930s. The advertisement stated "Remember the Dixie is foolproof and rattle proof".

These two photographs show The Forge in 1905 with Mr Wothers on the doorstep in the view on the right. The Wothers' family lived here and worked the forge from around the mid 19th century, and it continued to be used as a blacksmith's until the 1970s. The furnace is still fully operational with tools and related items on display in the adjoining shoeing bay. The Forge is open for special events in the town, such as the Heritage Weekend.

The cottages in the foreground were thatched and originally comprised of six small dwellings, they now have tiled roofs and have been converted into three larger cottages. To the right of the picture is the Independent Chapel and adjacent Chapel House, built in the late 18th century. They were demolished in 1961 and replaced by two apartments which have now been converted into one dwelling.

These cottages once contained a cobbler's workshop, newsagents and a tuck shop. The tuck shop was very popular with the children attending St Peter's Primary School opposite. Newspapers were collected early each morning from the railway station in a box on wheels by Mrs Cooper. A notice by the door states that they were also agents for Pullars Dyeworks in Perth.

This view of Park Street taken in 1923 shows the primary school on the left, in front of which is a village pump, with children congregated around it. This is just one of many pumps located in the village. One remains in situ at the top of Sutton Lane. These cottages and the old primary school are Grade II Listed Buildings.

St Peter's Primary School was built in 1848 and was the only school in the town, apart from the Dixie Grammar School. Both photographs date from the early 20th century. The architectural style reflects many of Market Bosworth's 19th century buildings. It was used as a primary school until 1974 but is now two residential properties retaining much of their original character.

To the left of the photograph is the English Master's house, built on land once owned by the Free Grammar School and used as allotments. An engraving on one of the windows states: "Came to this house August 1836". The house is in the Tudor style to mirror the Grammar School building and is close to the site of the Medieval school. It is of white East Anglia brick and a three-storey Grade II Listed Building. It was built for John Edwards who was English Master at the Dixie Grammar School in the early 19th century.

This is an aerial photograph of Church Walk taken in June 1970 showing St Anne's Lodge, the school Nissen hut top left.

St Anne's Lodge was an extension of the primary school, used mainly by the reception class. The building was a wartime Nissen hut located at the top of Church Walk. It has now been demolished and the new Rectory built on the site. These photographs, and those over the page, were taken in the early 1950s. Many of the children still reside in the locality.

Views of Church Walk off Park Street.

This photograph, looking down Park Street in the early 20th century, illustrates how much property has been demolished. The attractive cottage on the left with the decorative bargeboard, the Independent Chapel, Chapel House and the cottages in The Dixie Arms Hotel yard entrance have now gone. On the right adjacent to The Forge was Stanton's orchard now replaced by St Peter's Parish Hall built in the 1930s and extended in the 1950s. To the extreme right is the English Master's House, built in the 1830s, complete with railings.

This photograph of The Inn on the Park was taken in 1988. The portion of land on which it was built was sold to a Birmingham business man in the early 1930s. It was he who built the Neo-Georgian house which became Bosworth Field Restaurant, and latterly The Inn on the Park. It was the home of the Dixie family until the early 1980s when Lady Dixie moved away from Market Bosworth, Sir Wolstan having died in December 1975. It has now been demolished and replaced by detached houses.

The Old Rectory was built in 1849 on the site of The Old Bowling Green Close and was the home of the local rector until 1986 when it was sold. The rear terraced garden seen in the photograph over the page is on the site of the old Bowling Green. The design mirrors the Elizabethan style of other buildings in the town with a Tudor porch similar to that of the Dixie Grammar School. Viewed from the curved front drive the servants' quarters are clearly defined to the right of the main building. The house is now a Grade II listed private residence.

The annual church fete and other events were traditionally held in the Rectory gardens. Below is a poster for the 1892 Bazaar and American Fair that was held in the Rectory grounds in aid of the Parish Church Organ Fund.

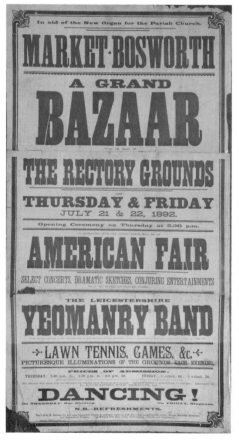

It was at the Parish Meeting in October 1891 when the decision to provide a new organ for the church, at a cost of £600, was agreed. An amount of £620 was raised through donations and takings on the day. Mr Thomas Cope of Osbaston Hall opened the event. The funds, £693, paid for the reredos, pulpit, chancel screen, altar rails, statues of St Peter and St Paul and a Litany desk. Before the days of political correctness the Bosworth Minstrels gave several performances throughout the day. In the evening the Rectory garden was illuminated by Chinese lanterns and coloured lamps, with dancing to the music of the band.

The old Bowling Green Close is mentioned on the 1848 Tithe map and, before the building of the rectory in 1849, one of the actual greens was sited in what is now the old rectory lawn. The photograph above is of the opening of the new bowling green pavilion in 1958.

CATTLE MARKET

Cattle Market, Market Bosworth

Above are two photographs of the Cattle Market during the ownership of Messrs Orchard & Joyce in the early 20th century. The saleground finally passed to Hackney & Son and closed in February 1996 after 135 years of business. Market Mews and the public car park now occupy the site.

This view of Rectory Lane, once known as Biggin Lane, shows Bakery Cottage, and adjacent to it, 4 Rectory Lane. The latter property was once a nail maker's workshop, which in 1895 was rebuilt by Charles Tollemache Scott as an estate house for the use of the gamekeeper. It is an attractive half-timbered property with a single gable and ornate barge boards.

It is thought that part of the property above dates from the 16th century. It was, at one time, a bakery and a farm. At the end of Bakery Cottage a shop window display can be seen. The smaller building on Sutton Lane to the right of the photograph was the actual bakehouse. This was damaged by fire in May 1932 and demolished in the 1950s. It is thought that the name Biggin Lane was derived from the name The Big Inn, which was an inn located in what is now Bakery Cottage.

This view looking up Sutton Lane, towards the bakehouse, is dated 1922. The Grade ll Listed Building on the right of the photograph dates from 1580 and was two properties at one time. It is a timber-framed dwelling with brick infill and a Norfolk reed thatched roof. Below is the same property during its re-thatching in 1966, the ridge was re-thatched in 1988.

This is an early 20th century photograph of 12 and 14 Sutton Lane when both properties had thatched roofs. Below is a similar view of the same cottages in the early 1950s showing the bakehouse before it was demolished. The group of local residents was asked by the photographer to stand in front of a recent delivery of loose coal which would have detracted from his photograph! The only addition to the properties is the lean-to at the end of No 14. The raised pavement is still in place today.

Sutton Lane, Market Bosworth.

These two views are of Sutton Lane at the gate, where the road leads to and from Sutton Cheney, enclosing the pasture land used for grazing cattle. To the left, in the above view, is the house built by Beck & Son in 1928, the garden of which adjoins the Old Rectory.

Below, the view looks towards the town centre with a 1930s property on the left. Beyond this is The Mount built in 1908, as stated in the sale advertisement illustrated to the right, detailing the auction at the Red Lion Hotel.

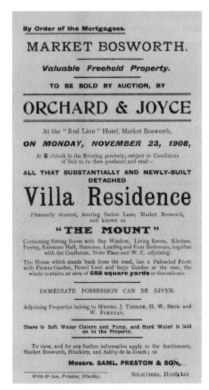

By Order of the Mortgagees.

MARKET BOSWORTH.

Valuable Freehold Property.

TO BE SOLD BY AUCTION, BY

ORCHARD & JOYCE

At the " Red Lion " Hotel, Market Bosworth,

ON MONDAY, NOVEMBER 23, 1908,

At 5 o'clock in the Evening precisely, subject to Conditions of Sale to be then produced and read—

ALL THAT SUBSTANTIALLY AND NEWLY-BUILT
DETACHED

Villa Residence

Pleasantly situated, fronting Sutton Lane, Market Bosworth, and known as

" THE MOUNT "

Containing Sitting Room with Bay Window, Living Room, Kitchen, Pantry, Entrance Hall, Staircase, Landing and Four Bedrooms, together with the Coalhouse, Store Place and W.C. adjoining.

The House which stands back from the road, has a Palisaded Front with Flower Garden, Paved Yard and large Garden at the rear, the whole contains an area of **688 square yards** or thereabouts.

IMMEDIATE POSSESSION CAN BE GIVEN.

Adjoining Properties belong to Messrs. J. Thorpe, H. W. Beck and W. Foreman.

There is Soft Water Cistern and Pump, and Hard Water is laid on to the Property.

To view, and for any further information apply to the Auctioneers, Market Bosworth, Hinckley, and Ashby-de-la-Zouch; or

Messrs. SAML. PRESTON & SON,

With & Son, Printers, Hinckley.   SOLICITORS, HINCKLEY.

Here is a view of three Victorian terraced cottages, built on the site of earlier dwellings by Charles Tollemache Scott, as estate houses. They have the characteristic elaborate chimney stacks of the Estate architecture with timber and tiled facades.

SHENTON LANE

This charming photograph of Rainbow Cottage, Grade II listed, shows a little girl, probably with her grandmother, by one of the village pumps. The pump still exists today and is also Grade II listed. It dates from the early 19th century and is made of cast iron with decorative panels. Rainbow Cottage is of cruck construction dating from the 16th century.

Rainbow Cottage is one of the oldest properties in Market Bosworth built on an earth foundation with a Carlton stone plinth.

This view of Shenton Lane illustrates early 20th century buildings with the two late Victorian villas on the left of the picture. Rainbow Cottage is just visible in the middle distance.

On the corner of Warwick Lane stands the imposing Lindley House and next to it Beaumont House built by H W Beck & Son. They were built around 1900 on his land which had previously been used as a timber yard.

The new Police Station was located in Shenton Lane in 1896. It replaced the old Police Station in Back Lane (now Warwick Lane) and is in the style of the 17th century architecture of Bosworth Hall.

The Magistrates' Court and the new Police Station were built in 1896. The Dixie Grammar School have used the old court building as an Art Department since the early 1990s.

W A R W I C K   L A N E

Warwick House, the old Police Station, was built in 1847. The architectural style reflects the Estate buildings of the 19th century and the Dixie Grammar School. The cells and courtroom can still be identified.

Looking west from the Market Place along Station Road, once called Litchfield Street, is a row of three-storey listed buildings which have 16th century stone-built rear walls. The frontage is early 19th century and No 7 has a Regency style bow window of that period. This row of houses, centered around Glebe Farmhouse, all belonged to the Glebe at one time. The view below looking towards the Market Place shows members of the Quincey family standing next to the old wall of the Dixie Grammar School which was demolished to make room for the erection of the school hall in 1938.

The chapel above right, is hidden behind 7, 9 and 11 Station Road. The chapel was built by the Baptists in 1794 and was in use until 1848 when the present Free Church was built on Barton Road. Access to it was probably via an alleyway adjacent to Softley's Restaurant.

The saddler's shop, owned by T Edgeley, was probably located close to the King William IV public house and shows Mr Edgeley in his shop doorway in the late 1890s. The number of collars, brasses and bits is an indication of the importance of the horse at this time.

The present King William IV public house was built in 1938 and replaced the building illustrated above, which probably dates from the early 19th century, as it was named after King William IV who reigned from 1830 to 1837. To the left of the pub was a barber's shop.

This row of eight three-storey cottages, to the rear of the King William IV public house, was equipped with knitting frames during the 1820s and 1830s when there was a flourishing stocking industry in the town. The frames were 6ft x 4ft x 3ft so must have dominated the upper storeys. An early hosiery factory was also located in this area. These buildings were demolished in the late 1930s. The bunting was to celebrate the Silver Jubilee of King George V and Queen Mary.

1937 saw the demolition of the old King William IV public house.

A view looking up Warwick Lane with Jubilee Terrace on the left and 4 Warwick Lane on the right.

Kelly's Garage was, until 1973, managed by Maurice Kelly,
with his brother Jim running a barber's shop next door.

The garage and petrol station was purchased by Ken and Vivienne Coleman in 1973 and, as the picture illustrates, some improvements and extensions were added. The photograph shows Jaguar and Bentley cars on their way to a local rally. The business has since been transferred to a site close to the railway and is now a repair garage known as Station Garage. Four houses have now been built on this site.

The Wembley houses were relocated here following their use at the Wembley Exhibition in 1925 and were demolished for development of the site in the late 1990s. A Bentley car can be seen on the forecourt.

This is a view of Station Road looking east, with the new King William IV public house in the middle distance, and the wooden Wembley houses to the right, demolished in the 1990s. Kelly's Esso petrol station and garage can just be seen. Aylesbrook Cottage, built in the 17th century, on the immediate left, is thatched with long wheat straw. Adjacent to this is Coleman's coal merchant's.

In the centre of the photograph at the top of the page is Mr & Mrs Granger's thatched cottage, a closer view is seen above, and was originally two cottages. Standing around the motorbike watching tools being sharpened are Mr & Mrs Granger with Larry Gains who trained at The Dixie Arms Hotel and was a heavy-weight boxer in the 1930s. The motorbike is a 1926 Royal Enfield with a Bradshaw oil-cooled engine which was needed to operate the grindstone. The cottage was demolished in the late 1950s.

The Rural District Council offices above were built in 1931. Council members are seen alongside the RDC's fire brigade engine (Reg: BUT 146) of that period.

This photograph shows where the fire engine and dustcarts were garaged to the rear of the council offices. Note the Wembley houses on the left of the photograph and the squash courts adjacent to the RDC offices. The old Westhaven (the workhouse) buildings can be seen on the far right.

"Post Proelia Concordia"
After the battle concord.

The Rural District Council's Coat of Arms, granted in 1954, was acquired at a presentation by the Chairman of the County Council in February 1955. It can now be seen above the entrance to the HSBC Bank in the Market Place.

The Council building was constructed by local builder Mr Beck, and like other of his designs, the building is adorned by balustrades, pillars and gables. The Bosworth & Hinckley Councils merged in 1972 when authority was transferred to Argents Mead, Hinckley. The building is now Bosworth Court Care Home where they have approximately forty residents.

Westhaven, Market Bosworth.

The Union Workhouse was built in 1836 as a result of the Poor Law Commission in 1832. It cared for the sick and elderly for more than one hundred years. The Board Room is to the left - being built in 1905. The extent of the Workhouse can be seen behind the main buildings and these were constructed around four courtyards. It was in use until the 1960s when it underwent modernisation. Only the buildings fronting onto Station Road remain and were used as an elderly persons' home known as Westhaven before being converted into apartments. The buildings to the rear were demolished in 1979 after which the Fire Station and Westhaven Court were developed.

The original Sedgemere was a thatched cottage adjacent to the railway but sadly it was burned down in 1936 due to a spark from a passing goods train setting fire to the thatch. Mr Salmon had the house rebuilt with a tiled roof. The mere or lake was a shallow clay pit, close to the brick yard. Vibrations from bombs falling on Coventry in World War ll caused railway sleepers to be dislodged and float to the surface of the pond. Some of these were subsequently used in the building of a summer house.

Wharf Cottage, adjacent to Sedgemere, with
Mr Hodges on his BSA C10 motorbike in the
1920s or 1930s.

This picture illustrates the factory of the Timber Fireproofing Company Ltd, built in 1921. The Company moved from London and chose Market Bosworth as its new site due to its central geographic location and ease of transport by rail and canal. In 1975 there were 12 timber kilns and 9 plywood dryers. Timber on ships, aeroplanes and the London Underground have all been treated on this site. It was the largest factory of its type on one site, then, in the UK and probably in Europe.

In the foreground is the gasometer, a reminder of the gas plant that existed here. Gas came to Market Bosworth in the 1880s with the main user of this service being the Dixie Grammar School where some of the original fitments are still in place. This gasworks ended production around 1916.

The site has now become a housing development of nearly 100 dwellings, known as Waterside Mede.

This photograph shows part of the seven acre site where the timber was stored.

This photograph, taken around 1908, shows the entrance to the Station with the Stationmaster's House to the right of the picture.

The railway came to Market Bosworth in 1886 and was part of the London & North West & Midlands Counties Coalfield Railway. Market Bosworth Station was built in 1870. The stretch of line between Nuneaton and Moira, known as the ANJR, Ashby & Nuneaton Joint Railway, was completed in 1873 at a cost of £550,000. A celebration of the completion of the station, with brass band and picnic, was held in August of that year and the line opened to passengers on the 1st September. The station is a single-storey building with two large chimneys. A wooden covered veranda with cast iron pillars extended towards the platform was later replaced by brick. When the railway closed it became Station Garage.

This photograph of the platform side of the station shows a passing train in the foreground.

Here a gang of railway employees work on the points close to the station, with Joseph Ellis & Sons Coal Merchants behind and the engine sheds in the background.

Miss Hetty Lovell was a railway porter during the First World War having left school at 13. The above photograph was taken around 1915 when she was 22. The two station porters are wearing the distinctive uniform of the Ashby & Nuneaton Joint Railway.

Railway employees photographed in front of a steam engine transporting rocks with the Stationaster's House situated left of the station. The line was finally closed to all traffic in 1971 and the track removed the following year. However, the Shackerstone Railway Society restored the line between Shenton and Shackerstone and it now operates as the Battlefield Line.

Market Bosworth Station in 1965 playing host to an Aveling & Porter traction engine in the foreground and an engine owned by local farmer, John Vernon of Newbold Verdon, in the background.

The 18th century saw the development of many canal systems and it was in 1792 that a meeting was held in Ashby de la Zouch to discuss the Moira Cut or the Ashby Canal as it is known today. The idea was well supported, despite the objection of local landowners. By 1794 plans were drawn up and construction of the canal began in October. By 1804 the 14ft wide waterway was completed. The canal reached Market Bosworth in 1798, a warehouse with living accommodation was built just north of Market Bosworth bridge (No 42) by a local trader Joseph White. It was built to accommodate the increasing need to transport coal. The warehouse building was demolished in 1959.

The warehouse viewed from
the canal

The Canal, Market Bosworth

Market Bosworth canal bridge.

The present building dates from the 14th and 15th centuries but there was a Saxon church on the site prior to that time. The tower is the oldest part of the church having been started in 1325. The original roof was probably thatched and the steeper pitch is visible in the stonework on the west wall. The present roof and corbels date from the 19th century.

Bosworth Church   W. Shepherd & Co.'s Series   40438

This recent painting of the Old Parsonage, by Steve Dilks, was based on an earlier line drawing. The Parsonage, built at the end of the 17th century, was once reckoned to be one of the finest in England. The building was in a poor state of repair in 1847 and was demolished.

Inside the main entrance to the church a drawing by Sebastian Evans shows the interior in 1847. The photograph shows the unattractive solid fuel heating system at that time. The curtained family pew was for the use of the local gentry from Bosworth Hall and Osbaston Hall. It was later removed and the Dixie pew located in its present position next to the doorway in the north aisle. The pews were installed in 1845 and the chancel screen and reredos during the later Victorian period.

The photograph is of Canon Payne, Rector of Market Bosworth from 1931-1954. The occasion is the re-dedication of the bells in April 1950. Five of the bells are very old, three of them being dated 1624, 1630 and 1658. Three new bells were dedicated on this date in 1950. When they were added the five original bells had to be lowered by sixteen feet as the spire would not have stood the vibration at a greater height.

This interior of the church shows the addition of the Chancel screen and the pulpit in its new position. In the foreground is the font, which is the oldest item in the church, the base of which dates from the early 13th century.

Sir Arthur Wheeler, who had bought the Bosworth Estate in 1913, gave the land on which the present church stands, to the Catholic Church in 1931. The building work began on 12 March 1931, which was St Gregory's Day, but his feast day was moved to 3rd September in 1969. St Gregory I was consecrated as Pope on 3rd September 590AD. His name gave rise to the church music we know as "Gregorian Chant". The Victorian font is probably the oldest item in the church. The original church on Station Road was much smaller but extensions in 1975 and 1982 increased the capacity to accommodate 200 people.

MARKET BOSWORTH FREE CHURCH

Since the 18th century there have been non-conformist churches in Market Bosworth. Methodists worshipped at a church in Station Road, the Baptists too built a chapel in Station Road and at about the same time the Independents built a chapel in Park Street. These buildings have now been demolished with the exception of the Baptist Church off Station Road, which was used until 1848 when the new Baptist Church was built on Barton Road. This building was used for worship until 1936 at which time it was closed and fell into a state of disrepair but Baptists continued to meet in a room above the Central Cafe in the Market Place. During World War II the Barton Road chapel was used as a storage depot and after the war was abandoned again until 1949. Restoration of the building began at this time and the Free Church, as we know it today, was opened in 1951. At present a project to extend the building is in progress.

A survey in 1588 indicated a manor house on the present site of Bosworth Hall, possibly a moated manor house. This was demolished in the 1670s when the building of the present Hall commenced, initiated by the then baronet, Sir Beaumont Dixie. It took some ten years to complete this splendid brick and stone country house.

The Dixie family sold the Estate to Charles Tollemache Scott in 1885 but, on the death of his wife, Lady Agnes, the Estate passed to his daughter, Wenefryde, who did not wish to remain in Market Bosworth. The Estate was sold in 1918 and was bought by Mr Arthur Wheeler who later auctioned it off in lots. Mr Rudolph Delius bought the house in 1918. In 1931 he sold the house to Leicestershire County Council for £5,000 for development as a hospital which was opened in 1936. The main entrance gates, with the initials TS woven into the wrought iron, were sold separately for an additional £500. The Hall remained a hospital until 1987 when it was sold again for development as a country hotel. Britannia Hotels eventually opened the present Hall after much extension and alteration.

Above is a detail from a painting thought to be by the Flemish artist, Jan Siberechts. It shows Bosworth Hall in 1703, just after its completion.

This is an aerial view of Bosworth Hall during the period when it was the Infirmary. It opened as a hospital in 1936 and closed in 1987. In the foreground is Swan House which is now used as offices by small businesses.

The nurses' home was built in the late 1930s to accommodate some of the hospital staff. The style of building was designed to complement the Palladian architecture of the Hall. It has now been converted into ten appartments and is known as St Peter's Court.

This gateway, once at the corner of Park Street and The Park, was relocated to create the main entrance to the hotel.

Below is a view of the west front of the Hall showing the two beech trees, one of which was struck by lightning and blew down in 1974. The area in front of the Hall is now the main car park.

THE HALL, MARKET BOSWORTH.

A horse-drawn gig outside the main entrance to Bosworth Hall.

A view of the inner courtyard.

The Hall from the south side.

The photograph shows the oak panelled Entrance Hall with its black and white marbled floor and pargetted ceiling.

The grand Oak Staircase, with its ornate carving of baskets of fruit, leading to the top corridor.

Mowing the south lawn in the early 20th century.

A view of the south side of the Hall and the Water Tower from The Park taken in 1928.

A view of the Deer Park, now the Country Park, taken in 1920 when there was a herd of 200 to 300 animals. The only herd of black old-English fallow deer in existence, at that time, roamed here.

The photograph shows the Water Tower, two vinery glass houses, two peach houses and also several more glass houses for other exotic fruits. There was bothy accommodation for the employees. The Water Tower was built in the early 1880s by Charles Tollemache Scott to house a means of pumping water to the Hall, and is still used for that purpose today.

The summer house, now demolished, provided the entrance to the subterranean Ice House. In 1908 a heifer fell into the Ice House and was trapped for ten days without food before being rescued.

The Infirmary was opened in July 1932 with 177 beds for the chronically sick. It was used mainly for general post-operative care with operations only performed for the removal of tonsils. Later a unit was designed with its own physiotherapist for physically handicapped children - the only such unit in Leicestershire at that time. During World War II a maternity unit opened with 19 beds and reached a turnover of 500 babies per year.

The photograph above shows the Night Nursery which held, on average, ten children.

Nurses March, Elliot and Parry

Two large marine boilers supplied the complex with constant hot water and heat. These giants consumed sixteen tons of coal per week and were maintained by engineer, Mr A Loseby and stokers, one of whom, Mr L Pallet, is pictured above.

The Infirmary kitchen, 1938

Mr Douse with the first hospital van, in the early 1950s.

Staff at the Infirmary's 21st Anniversary celebration.

Staff at Westhaven with Mr & Mrs Allen (Matron) centre front in the 1950s. Some of the staff also worked at Bosworth Park Infirmary.

The East Lodge was built in the Queen Anne style by Charles Tollemache Scott in 1885. The initials CTS can be seen on the lead downpipes. Gables enhance each side of the Lodge and are of a Dutch design. The lodges were often occupied by the park keepers.

The gate piers date from the 17th century. The piers are still in existence but have had to be relocated to enable widening of the road.

Charles Tollemache Scott

Lady Agnes Tollemache Scott

Charles and Agnes' daughter, Wenefryde, on the left, after her
marriage to Mr Owain Greaves.

Canon P C Bowers

The wedding of Miss L B M Bowers 1911

A wedding party outside Lindley House, Shenton Lane with
Canon Bowers far right

Pupils at the Dixie Grammar School in the early 1900s.

Rev A Benoni Evans appointed Headmaster of
the Dixie Grammar School in 1829

Mr W F Gosling - Headmaster
of the Dixie Grammar School
1944-1964

The Graver family are pictured in Church Walk and outside the English Master's House. Mr R G Graver was Headmaster of St Peter's C of E School, Park Street from 1896 until he died in 1926 when his son, Gilbert, took over and later went on to become Headmaster of the Secondary Modern School in 1927, before retiring in December 1957. Miss Tapp took over the headship of the junior school after Mr Graver left, being Headmistress until 1947, when she retired.

Class 2 at St Peter's Junior School in 1900/01. Headmaster, Mr Robert G Graver with his wife, Elizabeth Lucy, are on the right.

A St Peter's Primary School photograph 1928-29.

A St Peter's Primary School play in the mid 1950s.

Mrs Fisher with pupils from St Peter's Primary School. The church weathercock
was taken down for maintenance in the 1950s.

Mr Frost and Mrs Fisher with girls from the Primary School in the mid 1950s.

The netball team at the Secondary Modern School, Station Road, in the mid 1950s.

The Food Office staff outside their headquarters at the Scout Hut during World War II.

Sid Folwell from The Dixie Arms Hotal with servicemen home on leave during the
1940s - Jim Hicklin, Les Calver, Len Harris, Joe Cheshire and George Armson.

'B' Company 8th Bn of The Leicestershire Home Guard, Market Bosworth
Division during 'The Stand Down' of the Guard in November 1944.

The girls of the Women's Land Army based at the Market Bosworth hostel in 1947-48.

The West Yorkshire Regiment in the Market Place, 1914.

Some customers outside Ye Olde Red Lion Hotel.

A group of employees from George Oliver Boot & Shoe Company's
outing, in front of The Dixie Arms Hotel, 1904.

The Parliamentary candidate, Mr Stoneham, on Nomination Day, January 1906, in a 1904 Darracq car.

The Bosworth ladies on a bus outing with driver, Mr Collins, in the early 20th century.

The Mothers' Union in the Rectory garden in 1925.

A photograph of the Trivett family taken outside Ye Olde Red Lion Hotal in the early 1900s.

An early drama production in St Peter's Parish Hall.

The Quincey's delivery cart.

This photograph was taken on the occasion of the opening of St Peter's Hall which was built mainly from public subscription, by H Beck & Son in 1938.

Mr S Folwell raising the flag at the Bowling Green on the new pole, circa 1953.

The presentation of the Rural District Council's Coat of Arms in 1955.

A photograph of Beck & Son's builder's yard, which is now Warwick Close.

Some of Beck & Son's work force.

The Atherstone Hunt meeting in the Market Place in 1918 with Mrs Inge, Master of the Atherstone Hunt, riding side saddle outside Richmond House.

The Game Cart used to collect the day's bag on the Bosworth Estate in 1906.

The Atherstone Hunt with hounds and keen supporters in the late 20th century.

Local farmers at a sale at the Cattle Market which closed in 1996. Market Mews was built on the site.

The Cattle Market was in existence for 331 years before its closure.

Sergeant J W Rawson lived with his family in the Police House from 1952 before retiring in 1963.

Roger Payne with his father, John Payne, and John Rawson (centre). Roger sold agricultural supplies at the Cattle Market.

Messrs Jarvis, Smith, Wain and Lampard enjoying a well-earned rest in the slaughter yard at the rear of Lampard's butchers shop in the early 1960s.

Mr French pegging out the washing outside his home in the Nissen hut in what is now The Dixie Arms Hotel car park.

Robert Jarvis, Bill Lancaster and Ashley Garratt in their medieval costumes for the Battle of Bosworth Quincentenary celebrations in 1985, at the rear of Lampard's butchers shop.

A crowd gathers outside W Shepherd's cycle shop in Park Street after the fire in July 1907. T Curtis's grocery shop can just be seen in the background.

Clem Phillips was the blacksmith at The Forge in Park Street from 1933 to 1972. Some of his numerous show certificates are displayed on the wall. He was Champion Farrier at the Royal Show in 1950 and 1963.

Brian and Glynis Oakley bought The Forge in 1997 and Brian was photographed here at one of the open days when the forge was fired-up for exhibition purposes.

A section of the crowd in the grandstand at the Market Bosworth
Agricultural Show, held in the Show Field, Brier Hills, August 1904.

The Bosworth Show, as it is now called, has been held annually since 1896 - except for the war
years and 2007, when the ground was waterlogged. The Show included stock, a flower show, fur
and feather and athletics until 1967. Since then the main focus has been on horse related events.

A photograph of one of the annual church fetes held in the Rectory
gardens in the early 20th century.

The Mayor of Hinckley & Bosworth Borough Council witnessing the burial of the Millennium
Capsule by members of the Parish Council, Community College and local residents, in the Parish
Field in the year 2000.

Market Day in Market Bosworth in the late 20th century.

Market Bosworth Rural District Council and Board of Guardians 1899 - 1901
T Cope - Chairman   C Tollemache Scott and N Drackley - Vice-Chairmen

Market Bosworth Parish Council 2008
Harry Whitehead - Chairman   Dick Symonds - Vice-Chairman